D0819641

STARTING SCIENCE

FLOATING

AND

SINKING

KAY DAVIES
AND
WENDY OLDFIELD

Steck-Vaughn
L I B R A R Y
A Division of Steck-Vaughn Company

Austin, Texas

Starting Science

Books in the series

Animals
Electricity and Magnetism
Floating and Sinking
Food

Light
Sound and Music
Waste
Weather

About This Book

This book investigates the forces that govern whether an object floats or sinks. Children are introduced to water as an environment for plants and animals. Activities with floaters and sinkers are included to encourage children's interest in the behavior of materials and water.

Floating and Sinking provides an introduction to methods in scientific inquiry and recording. The activities and investigations are designed to be straightforward but fun, and flexible according to the abilities of the children. Some will also involve the children in thinking about good designs. The main picture and its commentary may be taken as an introduction to the topic or as a focal point for further discussion. Each chapter can form a basis for extended topic work.

Teachers and parents will find that in using this book, they are reinforcing the other core subjects of language and mathematics. By means of its topical approach *Floating and Sinking* covers the following subjects usually taught in the early grades—exploration of science, the variety of life, types and uses of materials, and forces.

Editors: Cally Chambers, Susan Wilson

Typeset by Multifacit Graphics, Keyport, NJ
Printed in Italy by Rotolito Lombarda S.p.A., Milan
Bound in the U.S. by Lake Book, Melrose Park, IL
1 2 3 4 5 6 7 8 9 0 LB 96 95 94 93 92

Library of Congress
Cataloging-in-Publication Data

Davies, Kay.
  Floating and sinking / Kay Davies and Wendy Oldfield.
    p.   cm.—(Starting science)
  Includes index.
  Summary: Text, pictures, and suggested experiments introduce the forces that determine whether an object floats or sinks.
  ISBN 0–8114–3001–4
  1. Floating bodies—Juvenile literature.
2. Floating bodies—Experiments—Juvenile literature. [1. Floating bodies—Experiments.
2. Experiments.] I. Oldfield, Wendy. II. Title. III. Series: Davies, Kay. Starting science.
QC147.5.D38 1992   91-25756
532'.2--dc20   CIP AC

CONTENTS

Words that first appear in **bold** in the text or captions are explained in the glossary.

The aquarium makes a watery home for plants and animals.
We can look into their colorful world through the glass.

UNDERWATER WORLD

Look at all the things in this **aquarium**. Can you find their names in the **key**?

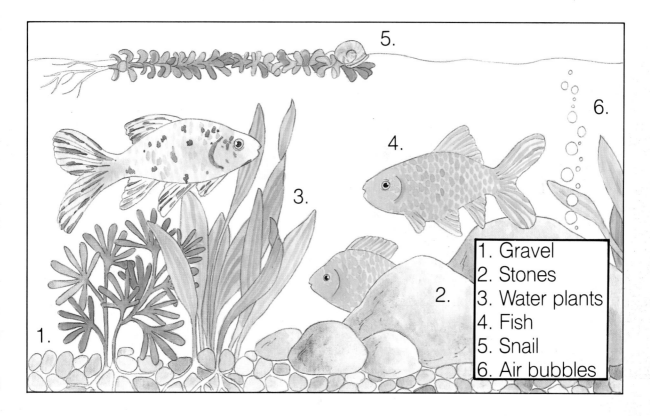

1. Gravel
2. Stones
3. Water plants
4. Fish
5. Snail
6. Air bubbles

Some things are at the bottom of the tank.
Some things are floating at the top.

The plants on the bottom have roots in the **gravel**.
The roots of some plants have come loose and can
no longer hold the plants down. These plants float.

The fish swim anywhere they like. Air is pumped into
the water for them to breathe. Do the air bubbles float up
or do they sink to the bottom?

ON THE BOTTOM

Collect some things that you think will sink.

Test them in water to see if you guessed right.

Use a tank with clear sides. You can watch your sinkers.

Make a chart like this to record your results.

Object	I guess it will–	Did it float?	Did it sink?	Was I right?
Stone	sink	no	yes	yes
Marble	sink	no	yes	yes
Apple	sink	yes	no	no

Do all your sinkers go straight to the bottom?

Now test a flat shell or a lid from a jar. Drop it in the tank and watch how it sinks.

Can you find any other things that move in the water like this?

This boat has sunk. It is lying on the bottom of the sea.
Fish and plants have made it their home.

AT THE TOP

Collect things that you think will float.

Put your objects on the surface of the water.

Do they float?

How much of each floater is under the water?

Make a "Floating Fun" picture for the wall.

Paint a big picture of your water tank.

Tape it to the wall.

Make pictures of your floaters and sinkers.

Cut them out and stick them on your water tank in the right place.

The **icebergs** are floating in the water.
Most of each iceberg is hidden underwater.

The fishing nets have been dropped in the water to catch fish.
The floats stop them from sinking to the bottom.

BOBBING UP AND DOWN

Can you use your floaters to keep your sinkers off the bottom?

Tape or tie a floater to each sinker.

Put them in the water to see what happens. Do all your sinkers still go to the bottom?

Watch your floaters to see what happens to them.

Can any of your floaters keep your sinkers off the bottom? Why do you think some floaters are better than others?

The **submarine** moves up and down underwater.
It sinks when the sailors let air out of special tanks.

AIR OUT, WATER IN

Float an empty plastic bottle in water.

Push it underwater. Watch the air bubbles escape from the bottle. Your floating bottle was *not* empty. It was full of air.

Does the bottle float when it is full of water?

Find things that have different size necks.

Test each one in water.
Which ones are quickest to let air out and water in?

BREAD AND WATER

Squeeze a loaf of bread and watch it spring back.

Drop a piece of bread in water. What happens to it?

Take the bread out and squeeze it. Is it still springy?

Squeeze a dry piece of bread into a ball. Drop it in the water. Does it sink right away?

When bread is springy and full of air, it soaks up water. Paper can soak up water, too.

Test some paper boats. Try using newspaper, a paper towel, wax paper, and wrapping paper.

Make all your boats in the same way.

Which boat floats the longest?

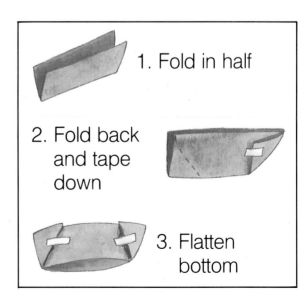

1. Fold in half

2. Fold back and tape down

3. Flatten bottom

The ducks and geese gobble up the bread before the pieces soak up water and sink.

SOGGY SPONGES

Squeeze a sponge and let it spring back into shape. Can you see the tiny air holes in the sponge?

Put it in water. Does it float or sink?

Pick up the sponge. Squeeze it and watch the water run out. Does it go back into shape?

Squeeze the sponge underwater. What comes out of it now?

Sponges can soak up lots of water. They are used for washing and mopping up spills. Natural sponges are animals. They live in water.

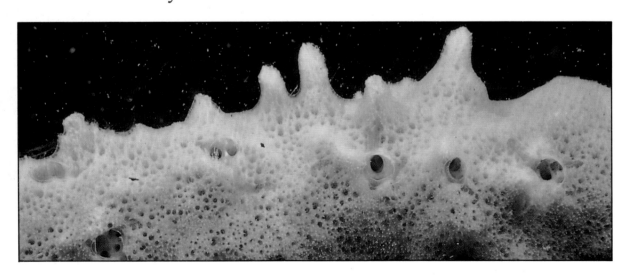

The family is using sponges to wash the car. The sponges soak up plenty of soapy water from the pail.

The air mattress and the water wings are full of air.
They help the girl float in the swimming pool.

FLOATING ON AIR

Blow up a balloon. Blow just a little air into another one.

Float the small balloon on water. Hold it under. Then let it go and see what happens.

Do this again with the big balloon. Which balloon is harder to push down?

Try these three ways of sinking a cup. Which is the hardest? Can you feel something pushing it back up?

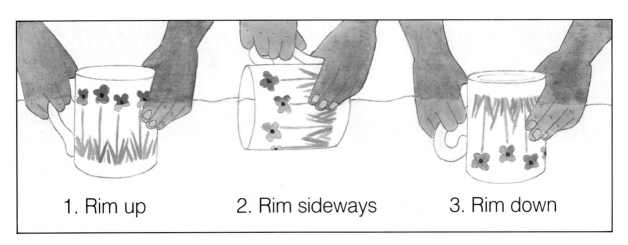

1. Rim up   2. Rim sideways   3. Rim down

Find other things that are hard to push underwater. Do they all have air trapped inside them?

MAKING A SPLASH

Set an empty fish tank in a sink or dishpan. Fill the tank to the top with water.

Lower a brick into the tank. What happens to the water?

Take the brick out. Is your tank still full to the top?

When the brick was in the tank, it pushed water out of the way. The water flowed out of the tank.

Half fill a large jar with water. Mark the side to show where the water comes to.

Put some floaters and sinkers in the jar, one at a time.

Do all the objects make the water rise higher?

The children are having fun in the wading pool. When they climb in, the water gets higher.

The boat has been made so that it floats well.
The people keep dry and enjoy their ride.

BEST BOAT

Test a ball of clay to see if it sinks or floats.

Make some clay boats with different shapes. Try round and long shapes. See if they will float.

Try high and low sides. Which of your clay boats floats best?

Make some more boats. Use aluminum foil, cardboard, wood, paper, plastic, or plastic foam.

Which boats float well? Do any boats not float at all? You may have to try out different **designs**.

ROCK AND ROLL

Boats can carry **cargo** and people.

Make a boat out of clay or aluminum foil. Use marbles as your cargo. Count them into your boat.

Watch the boat as your marbles go in.

What happens if you put too many marbles in your boat?

Boats have to be loaded carefully. They cannot carry too much. They might sink in stormy seas.

The men are bringing their fish back in their canoe. They have to be careful if they stand up in their wobbly boat.

The sailboats lean over in the wind. Their keels help keep them from tipping over.

KEEPING UPRIGHT

This toy boat has a **keel**.

It is attached to the **hull** of the boat.

It helps to keep the boat upright.

Hull ——— Keel

Any floater can be made to balance better. To do this, something heavy needs to be attached to the bottom.

Drop a cork in water and watch how it floats.

Ask an adult to make holes in both ends of it. Push plastic straws into the holes.

Add a ball of clay to one straw and a sail to the other.

Does the cork float upright now? If not, use a bigger ball of clay.

WALKING ON WATER

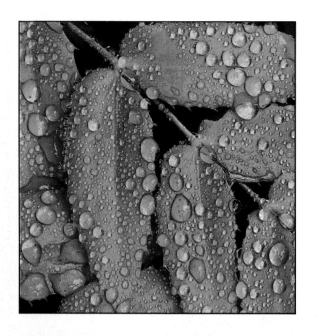

The surface of water has a strong **force**. This is called **surface tension**.

It pulls drops of water into round shapes like balloons.

It makes a kind of skin on the surface of the water.

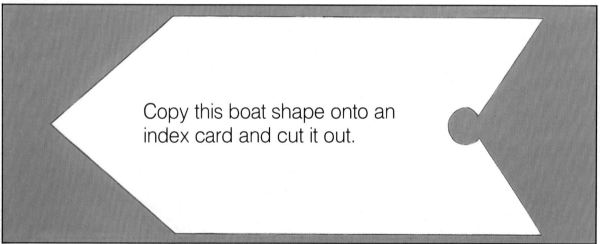

Copy this boat shape onto an index card and cut it out.

Gently float your boat on fresh, clean water. Drop a small spot of dishwashing liquid in the hole at the back. Watch your boat move.

The soapy liquid breaks the pull of the water behind the boat. The boat moves forward.

The small **pond skater** can walk on water. Its tiny, flat feet do not
break the surface tension.

GLOSSARY

Aquarium   A tank of water for fish and plants to live in.

Cargo   Goods carried by boats or ships.

Design   The way something is made.

Force   Strength or power.

Gravel   A mixture of small stones.

Hull   The main body of a boat or ship.

Iceberg   A big lump of ice floating in the ocean.

Keel   The part under a boat that helps it to balance in the water.

Key   A list that tells you what is in a picture.

Pond skater   A small insect that walks on water.

Submarine   A ship that can travel below the water's surface.

Surface tension   A force that pulls drops of water together making a skin on the surface.

FINDING OUT MORE

Books to read:

* **Floating and Sinking** by Terry Jennings (Gloucester, 1988)
* **Floating and Sinking** by Henry Pluckrose (Franklin Watts, 1987)
  Going Swimming by Celia Berridge (Random House, 1987)
  My Balloon by Kay Davies and Wendy Oldfield (Doubleday, 1990)
  Submarines by Kate Petty (Franklin Watts, 1986)
  Submarines by David Jefferis (Franklin Watts, 1990)
* **Water** by Brenda Walpole (Gloucester, 1987)

PICTURE ACKNOWLEDGMENTS

Barnaby's Picture Library 10; Biofotos (Heather Angel) 4; Cephas Picture Library 26; Eye Ubiquitous 18, 21; Greenpeace 7, 9; Hutchison Library 24; Frank Lane Picture Agency 29; Oxford Scientific Films 16 bottom, 28; Papilio 15; Planet Earth Pictures 12; Research House 25; Wayland Picture Library (Zul Mukhida) cover, 6, 8 both, 11, 13, 14, 16 top, 19, 20, 23 both, 24 top, 27; ZEFA 17, 22.
Artwork illustrations by Rebecca Archer. Cover design by Angela Hicks.

INDEX

First published in 1990 by Wayland
(Publishers) Ltd.
©Copyright 1990 Wayland (Publishers) Ltd.